THE STORY OF
HALLOWEEN

By Carol Greene

Illustrated by Linda Bronson

HarperCollinsPublishers

For Susan Bellville

—C.G.

To my mother, for all those
amazing costumes . . .

—L.B.

The Story of Halloween
Text copyright © 2004 by Carol Greene
Illustrations copyright © 2004 by Linda Bronson
Printed in the U.S.A.
Library of Congress Cataloging-in-Publication Data
Greene, Carol.
    The story of Halloween / by Carol Greene ; illustrated by Linda Bronson. — 1st ed.   p.   cm.
Summary: Explores the history of Halloween from the holiday's Celtic origins over 2000 years ago to
present-day celebrations, and provides spooky riddles and ideas for pumpkin art.
ISBN 0-06-027946-X — ISBN 0-06-029560-0 (lib. bdg.)   1. Halloween—Juvenile literature. [1. Halloween.
2. Holidays.] I. Bronson, Linda, ill. II. Title.   GT4965.G74 2004   394.2646—dc22   2003014960

rinning jack-o'-lanterns. Crowds of clowns, monsters, fairy princesses, and space travelers tramping through crunchy leaves. A chilly breeze tickling the back of your neck. Choruses of voices yelling, "Trick or treat!" And candy—lots of candy. That's Halloween.

Ghosts, druids, and singers. Hilltop fires blazing against a black velvet sky. Murmured prayers in an old graveyard. That's Halloween, too—the way it used to be.

he story of Halloween begins over 2,000 years ago. At that time, people known as Celts lived in Great Britain, Ireland, and northern France. October 31 was the last day of the year for them. They called it Samhain (pronounced "SOW-in"), which means "summer's end."

On Samhain, the Celts thanked the sun for their harvest and honored it with a fire ceremony. Each household put out the fire it had used for warmth and cooking during the previous year. The priests, called druids, rubbed dry oak branches together until they made sparks. The druids then used these sparks to light huge bonfires on nearby hills. Later, the head of each household would take embers from one of the bonfires home to start a new fire.

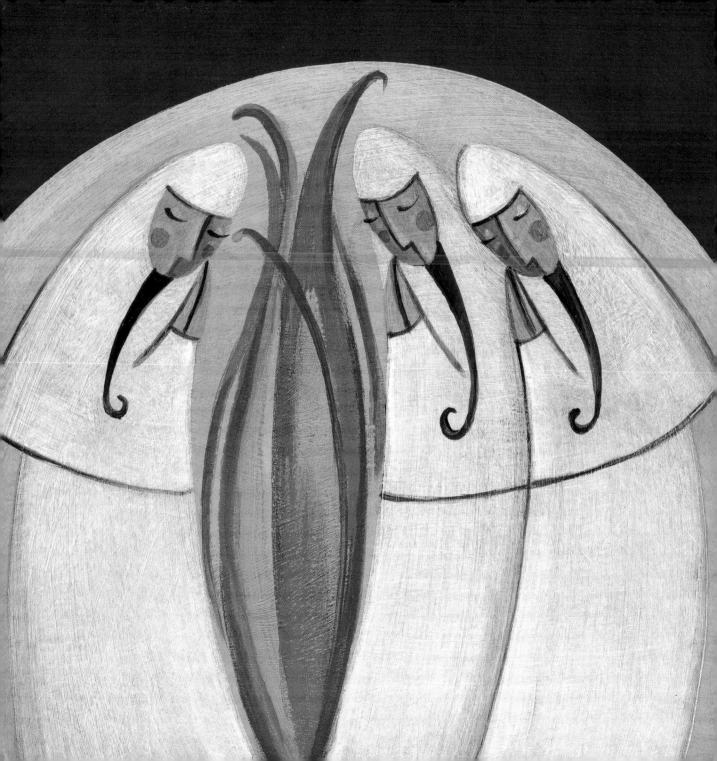

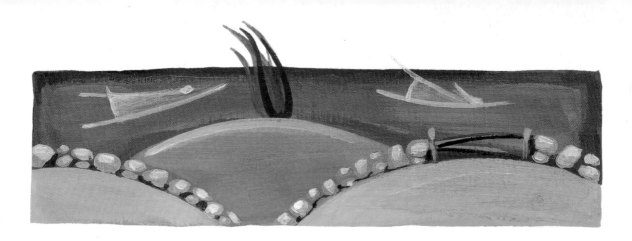

he Celts believed that their new fires, born from the bonfires' embers, would protect their homes during the coming year. But on Samhain itself, they counted on the bonfires for special protection. On Samhain, they believed, the ghosts of everyone who died during the past year came back with elves, fairies, and other scary creatures.

No one wanted to feel a ghostly hand touch them as they slept. No one wanted an elf to snatch their hair or a fairy to sour their milk. So they let the bonfires burn bright and hoped that so much light would frighten the spooks away.

n A.D. 43, the Romans conquered the Celts. The Romans held different beliefs, but they also celebrated a harvest ceremony around October 31. Their feast honored Pomona, their goddess of fruits. Since the Romans had just finished harvesting apples and nuts from the trees, they offered some of each to Pomona. This was their way of saying thank you, and of encouraging Pomona to give them a good crop again the next year.

Of course the Romans ate some of the apples and nuts, too. But they also used them to tell the future.

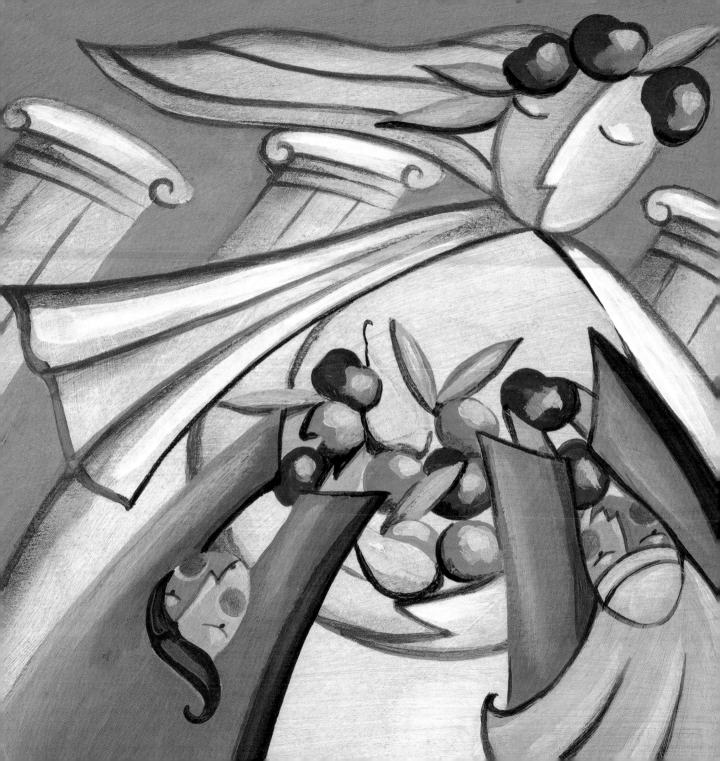

In the years that followed, Christian missionaries came to the Celts and told them about a different god. Gradually the Celts accepted their ideas until Christianity became the main religion of Great Britain. In the A.D. 700s, the Roman Catholic Church decided that November 1 would be named All Saints' Day, or All Hallows' (Holy Ones') Day, a time to remember and honor special people who have died. On the evening before, All Hallows' Eve, which was shortened to Halloween, people visited cemeteries and prayed for loved ones buried there.

But people in Great Britain still held on to some of their old ideas. Many, especially those who lived in the country, continued to believe that spooks wandered around on October 31, bothering their crops and animals. So they went on burning bonfires, telling scary stories, eating nuts and apples, and playing a game called "bobbing for apples."

n some parts of England, folks wandered from house to house begging for soul-cakes (currant buns), or a penny at least. They sang, "If you haven't got a penny, a half-penny will do. If you haven't got a half-penny, then God bless you!"

Not all of these old-time trick-or-treaters wanted soul-cakes or pennies, however. Some would rather make mischief. They traveled in groups, blocking up their neighbors' doors or covering their chimneys so the smoke would stay inside. Often they wore masks so their neighbors wouldn't know who they were, just as trick-or-treaters often do today. And if someone complained, they just said, "Oh, the spirits did it."

olks in Ireland also held on to some of the old traditions. Groups of people traveled from house to house asking for food and money, sometimes for the poor and sometimes for themselves. They promised good luck for the generous and trouble for the stingy. But while some did all this in the name of St. Columba, a Christian monk, others did it for Muck Olla, a druid god.

Instead of using regular lanterns to light up their All Hallow's Eve activities, the Irish often hollowed out large turnips, rutabagas, and potatoes. Then they carved ugly faces into the vegetables and stuck candles inside.

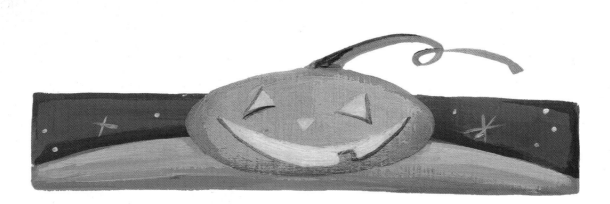

ne story the Irish brought to the United States told of a man from long ago named Jack. Jack was not a good man. He drank too much, and he wouldn't share anything with anyone.

"Jack's the stingiest man around," folks said.

Everyone knew Jack wouldn't get into Heaven. But after he played some dirty tricks on the Devil, he couldn't get into Hell, either. All he could do was wander around in the dark.

Eventually, even the Devil felt sorry for Jack. He gave Jack a glowing coal so he could see where he was going. Jack stuck it into a carved turnip and that became his lantern, a jack-o'-lantern ("Jack of the Lantern").

Americans substituted a local vegetable, the pumpkin, for Jack's turnip. There were plenty of pumpkins around in late October. They were easier to carve and they looked just right, grinning, on Halloween.

y the end of the 1800s, people all across America were celebrating Halloween. They especially liked trick-or-treating, a tradition that came partly from the Irish, who went around in masks asking for food and money, and partly from the English, who asked for soul-cakes and pennies.

Some mischievous Americans ignored the treats and just played tricks. Their neighbors might wake up on November 1 to find their windows soaped, their hay wagon on the roof, or their pigs shut up in the outhouse. And if someone complained, they just heard, "Oh, the goblins did it."

mericans also fell in love with costumes as part of Halloween, an idea that might have come from several different places. Some Irish wanderers wore masks, and sometimes boys dressed like girls and girls like boys. In England people wore costumes for Guy Fawkes Day, a holiday on November 5. And hundreds of years before Americans ever heard of Halloween, Europeans used to hold parades around their churches on All Hallows' Day, when some people dressed as saints, angels, or devils.

Maybe American trick-or-treaters just decided to dress up as ghosts, witches, goblins, and other frightening creatures because they *were* still frightening even after so many years. After all, a big part of Halloween today continues to be acting scary—or scared.

Unfortunately, some pranksters did real damage with their tricks. They broke streetlights, slashed car tires, and even set fires. People used to be afraid of spooky creatures on Halloween—now they had to be afraid of other humans. And it was no longer safe for young children to go trick-or-treating.

Community leaders talked about the problem. They knew how much people loved Halloween. They didn't want to stop celebrating it. But they had to do something to make it safer, especially for children.

Soon different communities came up with different solutions. In some, everybody who wanted to marched in one big parade. In others, schools, parks, and shopping areas held smaller parades for children. They often gave prizes for the best costumes.

Some storeowners cleverly figured out how to stop children from soaping other people's windows. They had children draw Halloween pictures and enter them in a contest. The winners could then color their pictures on big store windows.

n 1950, a group of Sunday school children near Philadelphia, Pennsylvania, collected seventeen dollars while trick-or-treating. They decided to send the money to the United Nations Children's Fund (UNICEF). UNICEF helps poor and sick children around the world.

Other people thought this was a great idea. Now millions of children in the United States trick-or-treat for UNICEF. Some get money *and* candy. They take the money to collection centers, where adults give them a party. The Irish who collected food and money for the poor centuries ago would be proud of these children today.

alloween parties have become another popular way to celebrate in the United States. And once again some of the traditions go way back.

Bobbing for apples in a tub of water and eating candy apples bring to mind the ancient Romans and their goddess of fruits, Pomona.

Ghosts and other creatures that frightened the Celts show up as costumes and decorations today. So do creatures such as owls, bats, and spiders, which scared people long ago because they come out at night.

A cheerful jack-o'-lantern in someone's front window is the descendant of a rutabaga, turnip, or potato in long-ago Ireland.

And when someone begins telling spooky stories at a Halloween party, he or she is doing the same thing others did in Great Britain hundreds of years ago.

 cloudy October night. No moon, no stars. The dog barks and you step outside. Brrr—it's chilly. Suddenly something brushes against your face. Is it a ghost—or just a spider web? You shudder.

The dog barks again. Now you see them, horrible, grinning faces coming toward you. No, they're just a bunch of carved-out vegetables with lights inside. But who are the people in masks carrying them? Why, they're your neighbors, collecting food and money.

Now everyone is talking and laughing. The dog is wagging his tail. You give your visitors some coins and apples—lots of apples.

Whatever year it is, happy Halloween!

PUMPKIN ART

Instead of a plain jack-o'-lantern, why not try something a little fancier?
(Be sure to have an adult help you with sharp knives and candles.)

PUMPKIN PERSON

Use three pumpkins, one small, one medium, and one large. Carve lids and scoop out innards for each, but carve a face only in the smallest. Discard medium and large lids and stack the pumpkins on top of each other, placing the largest on the bottom. You can also draw extra features, add stick arms, and anything else you can think of to make your pumpkin person come alive.

PUMPKIN TOTEM

Use several pumpkins about the same size and shape. Prepare them as you did for the Pumpkin Person, but carve a different face on each. Then stack them on a level surface.

NOISY PUMPKINS

Make several jack-o'-lanterns. Place them on a table or box that is covered with a cloth. Place a tape player under the table with a tape you've made of "pumpkin noises." They can howl, scream, rattle chains, say "Happy Halloween!" or even sing Halloween songs. Or they can tell *disghosting* riddles.

SPOOKY RIDDLES for HALLOWEEN

You might tell these riddles at a party or while trick-or-treating.
Or maybe you wouldn't dare!

What do all law-abiding spooks get before Halloween?
A haunting license.

What colors are the spook flag?
Dread, fright, and boo.

Which movie do spooks like best?
"Goon with the Wind."

What is a spook's favorite dessert?
I scream.

What kinds of flowers do spooks plant in their gardens?
Marighouls and chrysanthemummies.

What do spook roosters say?
Cockadoodleboo!

What are large spooks with trunks called?
Elephantoms.

What do spooks think about these riddles?
Disghosting!